Rockin' On the Milky Way

by

Jean Lenox Toddie

FOUNDED 1830

NEW YORK HOLLYWOOD LONDON TORONTO

SAMUELFRENCH.COM

Copyright © 2008 by Jean Lenox Toddie

ALL RIGHTS RESERVED

CAUTION: Professionals and amateurs are hereby warned that *ROCKIN' ON THE MILKY WAY* is subject to a royalty. It is fully protected under the copyright laws of the United States of America, the British Commonwealth, including Canada, and all other countries of the Copyright Union. All rights, including professional, amateur, motion picture, recitation, lecturing, public reading, radio broadcasting, television and the rights of translation into foreign languages are strictly reserved. In its present form the play is dedicated to the reading public only.

The amateur live stage performance rights to *ROCKIN' ON THE MILKY WAY* are controlled exclusively by Samuel French, Inc., and royalty arrangements and licenses must be secured well in advance of presentation. PLEASE NOTE that amateur royalty fees are set upon application in accordance with your producing circumstances. When applying for a royalty quotation and license please give us the number of performances intended, dates of production, your seating capacity and admission fee. Royalties are payable one week before the opening performance of the play to Samuel French, Inc., at 45 W. 25th Street, New York, NY 10010.

Royalty of the required amount must be paid whether the play is presented for charity or gain and whether or not admission is charged.

Stock royalty quoted upon application to Samuel French, Inc.

For all other rights than those stipulated above, apply to: Samuel French, Inc., at 45 W. 25th Street, New York, NY 10010.

Particular emphasis is laid on the question of amateur or professional readings, permission and terms for which must be secured in writing from Samuel French, Inc.

Copying from this book in whole or in part is strictly forbidden by law, and the right of performance is not transferable.

Whenever the play is produced the following notice must appear on all programs, printing and advertising for the play: "Produced by special arrangement with Samuel French, Inc."

Due authorship credit must be given on all programs, printing and advertising for the play.

ISBN 978-0-573-66250-8   Printed in U.S.A.   #20718

No one shall commit or authorize any act or omission by which the copyright of, or the right to copyright, this play may be impaired.

No one shall make any changes in this play for the purpose of production.

Publication of this play does not imply availability for performance. Both amateurs and professionals considering a production are strongly advised in their own interests to apply to Samuel French, Inc., for written permission before starting rehearsals, advertising, or booking a theatre.

No part of this book may be reproduced, stored in a retrieval system, or transmitted in any form, by any means, now known or yet to be invented, including mechanical, electronic, photocopying, recording, videotaping, or otherwise, without the prior written permission of the publisher.

IMPORTANT BILLING AND CREDIT REQUIREMENTS

All producers of *ROCKIN' ON THE MILKY WAY* *must* give credit to the Author of the Play in all programs distributed in connection with performances of the Play, and in all instances in which the title of the Play appears for the purposes of advertising, publicizing or otherwise exploiting the Play and/or a production. The name of the Author *must* appear on a separate line on which no other name appears, immediately following the title and *must* appear in size of type not less than fifty percent of the size of the title type.

MOONBEAMS IN MID-MORNING

A COMEDY-DRAMA IN ONE ACT

CAST OF CHARACTERS

BARBARA – A middle age author and essayist.
WILLIAM – A poet on the skids.
CARLA – A reporter in her early twenties.

Scene

The action takes place in the Florida Everglades.

Time

The present

On stage an old wicker rocker sits left of stage center, a small stool down stage left. Up stage right is a large, colorful cardboard cut-out of a palm tree. Down stage right are cut-outs of swampy foliage in various shades of green.

At Rise: **BARBARA** *enters stage left carrying an old shotgun. A pretty woman, she wears khaki trousers, a colorful cotton shirt and waterproof boots. She lowers herself into the chair, sets the gun across her knees, closes her eyes and rocks. After a moment, startled by a rustling sound off stage right, she jolts upright and raises the shotgun.*

CARLA. *(Off-stage right.)* Oh!

BARBARA. Who is it?

CARLA. I'm caught in these… !

BARBARA. Speak up, or I'll blow you out of the water.

CARLA. *(Stumbles on stage pulling twigs from her hair. She wears a t-shirt, slacks and sneakers.)* It's me!

BARBARA. I'm me, you're you. And you're on private property!

CARLA. I'm sorry, but… *(Stamping her feet and pulling at her shirt.)* Look at me, I'm covered with gook and my feet are soaked! *(Looking up for the first time sees the raised shotgun.)* Hey! *(Backs up.)* I'm lost! I've been stumbling around in this… this swamp, or whatever! Look at me!

BARBARA. If the sight is distasteful close your eyes and open your ears. This is private property.

CARLA. I'm sorry. An old coot in town told me…. *(Looks around.)* But no! She couldn't be! Not out here! So creepy quiet and there's nothing…. *(Turning to* **BARBARA** *with a nervous grin.)* I'm from the south side. You know, noise. If I was stuck out here I'd wear a clove of garlic around my neck to scare away evil spirits.

BARBARA. Think of me as one of those evil spirits.

CARLA. *(Stares at* **BARBARA,** *digs into her knapsack, pulls out an old newspaper clipping, studies the clipping, then* **BARBARA.***)* Oh, my God, you're not her, are you? *(Looks again at the clipping.)* You mean I'm looking at...

BARBARA. *(Cutting in.)* You're looking at an ornery woman who takes pot shots at strangers!

CARLA. You are! You're Dr. Barbara Tyler!

BARBARA. Do I look like a doctor?

CARLA. No, but you look like this photograph.

BARBARA. Let me see that!

CARLA. *(Bobbing with delight.)* I've got me a scoop, haven't I? This little wop from the south side gone and got herself a scoop!

BARBARA. *(Returning the clipping.)* It's a rotten picture.

CARLA. It's from the Times!

BARBARA. It's not me.

CARLA. *(Checks the clipping.)* It's you alright. What do you do out here?

BARBARA. Enjoy the creepy quiet.

CARLA. *(Surveying the scene.)* But where do you...?

BARBARA. Brush my teeth and say my prayers? *(She points off stage left.)*

CARLA. You're kidding.

BARBARA. No.

CARLA. That hut?

BARBARA. That hut is home. No doorbell, no knocker, no visitors.

CARLA. *(Moves to stare off stage left. Spins around.)* Oh, I get it! Research! Another book! And disappearing like you did? A set-up, right? The wow buildup for publication? Not just brainy, brilliant! How many books is it now?

BARBARA. I assume even girls from the south side can count.

CARLA. I only have two hands. *(Scratches.)* And one of them is itching.

BARBARA. You've been plowing through Brazilian Pepper. Sap blisters the skin.

CARLA. Darn!

BARBARA. The glades aren't kind to snoops. Alligators and cottonmouth snakes take a toll.

CARLA. Oh, my god!

BARBARA. *(Taking a tissue from her pocket wipes the barrel of the shotgun.)* Slop around in those wet shoes and you'll get a fungus. *(Raises the gun.)*

CARLA. Have I done anything right?

BARBARA. No. Just been lucky.

CARLA. Lucky, alright. I can't believe I've found you. Nana's baby girl is one up on all those hot-shot reporters. *(Puts the clipping in a pocket an squats to take a small tape recorder from her knapsack unaware of the raised gun.)* I've got so many questions.

BARBARA. *(Aiming the gun over the palm tree.)* And I have no answers. *(Lowers the gun, aims at **CARLA**.)* As I said. This is private property!

CARLA. But you're a public person and... *(Looks up.)* Hey! *(**BARBARA** lowers the gun.)* Please, Dr. Tyler, people are dying to know...

BARBARA. What?

CARLA. Why you gave a wow of a speech on the mess we're making of the environment, then drove that dinky little car into the middle of the quad and blasted the windshield to smithereens.

BARBARA. Is that what happened?

CARLA. Weird, right? So why did you do it?

BARBARA. Why did she do it? *(Shrugs.)* A choice?

CARLA. Choice?

BARBARA. Herself or the windshield.

CARLA. Why would a woman with awards, honorary doctorates and essays in the Sunday Times stick a pistol in her mouth?

BARBARA. Probably made the mistake of giving up chocolate. Goodbye. *(Closes her eyes. Rocks.)*

CARLA. Dr. Tyler? *(No response.)* Dr. Tyler? *(No response.)* Please talk to me. Give me a break. A story like this... *(No response. Drops her knapsack, whispers.)* Dr. Tyler? *(No response. She plucks at her shirt, slumps to the ground and examines her feet.)* You're right. I'm going to get a fungus.

BARBARA. *(Sigh, opens her eyes.)* Who are you?

CARLA. Carla.

BARBARA. Is there a last name on your passport?

CARLA. I don't have a passport.

BARBARA. Did your daddy have a last name? Even on the south side people have a last name. A toilet that works? Perhaps not. But surely a last name.

CARLA. *(Jumps to her feet.)* Yes, I have a last name! A good old guinea last name! My last name is Manetti! Can a wasp wrap her tongue around that?

BARBARA. *(Studies the defiant young women.)* Good name. Be a good girl and go.

CARLA. I tried to get in touch, but you have no e-mail.

BARBARA. No e-mail.

CARLA. Or telephone.

BARBARA. Or telephone..

CARLA. Not even an address!

BARBARA. No mailbox.

CARLA. *(Pointing to the stool.)* Can I sit down?

BARBARA. Yes, you can, but, no, you may not.

CARLA. What?

BARBARA. You assume I'm Dr. Tyler, so assume I'm grammatically correct.

CARLA. Oh, come on, you're Dr. Tyler. That was your picture. Look, I've been sloshing around out there for more than an hour. I'm tired. *(Sets the stool beside the rocker.)* I need to sit down.

BARBARA. No.

CARLA. For a few minutes. *(Sits.)*

BARBARA. You're an impertinent young woman.

CARLA. They say you had a breakdown.

BARBARA. And a rude young woman.

CARLA. They say you were working too hard.

BARBARA. And too nosey for your own good! *(Raises the gun and squinting aims it over the palm tree.)*

CARLA. They say when you're well you'll fill auditoriums again.

BARBARA. This Dr. Tyler? How jolly. I wish the woman well.

CARLA. *(Frustrated, jumps to her feet, takes a turn around the stage.)* What do you do out here all day?

BARBARA. Weave baskets from palm fronds.

CARLA. You find that…

BARBARA. Rewarding? Very. If the unfortunate Doctor does the same she'll credit her recovery to the weaving of baskets from palm fronds.

*(**WILLIAM** enters stage left carrying large basket. A big attractive man in his early fifties he wears worn jeans, red sweat shirt, a yellow kerchief and waterproof boots.)*

WILLIAM. They're mucking up the water.

BARBARA. *(Rising.)* Drat 'em!

WILLIAM. Woa, relax. I scared them off. *(To **CARLA**.)* How do you do? *(Back to **BARBARA**.)* Been here two months and already a legend. *(To **CARLA**.)* Locals swear the glades are spooked. Ghostly old gal with a gun. *(Takes a flower from the basket, presents it to **BARBARA**.)* A blossom for my love. *(Takes a flower, tucks it behind **CARLA**'s ear.)* Another for our visitor. You find the most breathtaking orchids in the Everglades. My name is William. And you are?

BARBARA. Carla Manetti.

WILLIAM. Delighted.

CARLA. I'm here to interview Dr. Tyler.

WILLIAM. *(Looking around.)* Doctor… who?

CARLA. *(Pointing.)* Her.

WILLIAM. That lovely woman a doctor? What a bit of luck. And me with a blister on my bum.

CARLA. I write for The Herald.

WILLIAM. Ah, a reporter.

CARLA. Cub reporter, but on my way.

WILLIAM. I'm sure.

BARBARA. We had a chat. Now she's leaving.

WILLIAM. When I've just arrived? Surely not. I play an important part in this woman's life. That's why you're here isn't it? To tell the story of a beautiful woman who chooses to swat mosquitoes and bury her feet in the mud with the rest of us swamp rats?

CARLA. It's the story I'm determined to tell.

WILLIAM. Just so. *(Glances at* **BARBARA**.*)* Despite my appearance, young lady, I was once known to relieve myself in Fifth Avenue commodes. Yes, indeed. Now where shall we begin? In the middle, of course. Has she told you how she discovered me in New York City where I dined nightly on candied locusts and marinated artichoke hearts?

BARBARA. He imagines himself a poet. Locals encourage him.

CARLA. You're a poet?

WILLIAM. *(Sweeping bow.)* Once poet pet of the rich and infamous who filled my closet with velvet jackets and my pockets with gold pieces. Then along came she of tart tongue *(nods at* **BARBARA**.*)* who e-mailed me daily on my misplacement of commas. What could I do but bolt?

BARBARA. To my knowledge he has never used a comma.

WILLIAM. Now I find myself in the tropics where men don't wear socks and seldom wash their underwear, merely airing it out now and again. Happy as the proverbial lark with my initials carved in a table top at the D&D. And what does she do? She follows me. Can't get rid of her. I've tried bribery, of course. I've even promised to insert a few commas here and there, but she won't leave.

CARLA. *(Writing rapidly on a pad she takes from her knapsack.)* Wait till I catch up…. "airing out their underwear…"

BARBARA. I had no idea he was down here playing Englishman in the noonday sun. But since he is I'm sure there's a table at the D&D with his initials on it.

WILLIAM. *(Affecting an Irish accent.)* Irishmen drink a wee bit and Irish poets drink a wee bit more. Without a beer in my belly how am I to sing my song?

CARLA. You're kidding, right?

WILLIAM. I admit to having written a verse or two. What Irishman hasn't. *(Dramatically.)*

> "Shiva rested during the scorching hours
> in a valley far to the north
> cooling his toes in the mouth of his consort
> his lovely consort, Parvati."

CARLA. We studied that poem! How does it go? *(Mimics his dramatic delivery.)*

> "Evenings he strolled the streets unseen,
> a snake coiled round his neck,
> Holding a handkerchief to his nose
> and avoiding puddles of urine."

WILLIAM. My, my.

CARLA. You're William McPeak?

BARBARA. Don't be taken in. He may write a few jingles, but a poet? Please. He's a charming fabricator I first met in college.

WILLIAM. Don't be taken in. I tipped my hat to her before we were potty trained.

(They've embarked on a routine they enjoy.)

BARBARA. Friends.

WILLIAM. *(Insinuatingly.)* Close friends.

BARBARA. Class clown.

WILLIAM. Prom queen.

BARBARA. Squeaked through.

WILLIAM. Magna cum… something.

BARBARA. He lusted after every coed.

WILLIAM. Only you, my love, only you. I sat behind her in

English Lit. She wore a blouse the color of ripe apricots and there were moon beams in her hair, moonbeams in mid-morning.

BARBARA. No ambition.

WILLIAM. Enough for two.

BARBARA. Tossed his mortar board in the air and headed for the big city.

WILLIAM. She wrapped her mortar board in tissue and hopped a flight for Harvard.

BARBARA. He peppered the subway walls with graffiti.

WILLIAM. She aced every test.

BARBARA. And that Irish accent? Don't be fooled. He's a Jewish boy from Brooklyn.

WILLIAM. And her perfect diction? Don't be fooled. She was raised up in Hoboken.

BARBARA. He's not a poet.

WILLIAM. And she's not whoever it is you're looking for. You've stumbled upon two down 'n outs looking for a lost shaker of salt, as the song goes.

BARBARA. We're wasting your time and you're wasting ours. I have baskets to weave.

WILLIAM. And I have snail kites to count. *(To **BARBARA**.)* Beginning to see life in the water again, and Jimmy Knotts swears he's caught a glimpse of a panther.

BARBARA. I love that old gaffer's lies.

WILLIAM. Saw some spatterdock and white water lily on the way over.

CARLA. You must have practiced that routine. Well, I can play games, too. I was a street kid. *(Jerks a small camera from her knapsack, snaps a picture of **BARBARA**, spins around, snaps a picture of **WILLIAM**.)*

(Silence.)

BARBARA. Give me the camera.

CARLA. This little throw-away?

BARBARA. *(Raising the gun.)* Give it to me.

CARLA. Hold on a minute. *(Reaches into her pocket and pulls out a tape recorder.)* This has been on the whole time. It's all on tape. I was scribbling for effect.

BARBARA. I'll take them both. First the camera. Then the tape.

CARLA. You going to shoot?

BARBARA. If I must.

CARLA. So shoot. *(Turns with her back to* **BARBARA**, *wiggles her behind.)* Shoot me in the back. Shoot me in the back and you're guilty of murder.

BARBARA. I'm not going to kill you. I'm going to blow out your knees.

CARLA. You'll go to jail.

BARBARA. I said give them to me!

CARLA. *(Spinning around to face* **BARBARA**.*)* No!

BARBARA. Now!

CARLA. No!

*(***BARBARA*** takes aim.)*

WILLIAM. Enough! *(Crosses to Barbara, wrenches the gun from her hands, drops it on the ground. Crosses to* **CARLA**, *takes the camera and recorder, lays them in* **BARBARA**'s *lap.)*

CARLA. Damn you! *(Sinks to the ground, bangs a fist on the dirt.)* Damn you! *(Wipes her eyes with her fist smearing dirt on her cheek.)* It's not supposed to be like this! I'm a reporter! I'm not supposed to cry! Damn you both for making me cry!

WILLIAM. *(Takes a thermos from the basket. Wets his kerchief, raises* **CARLA** *to her feet, wipes her face.)* The lady over there is crackers.

CARLA. She's lying, isn't she? She is Dr. Tyler.

WILLIAM. Hard to tell.

CARLA. *(Removes the newspaper clipping from her knapsack, shows it to* **WILLIAM**.*)* See.

WILLIAM. A little blurry, might be her.

BARBARA. Might be, but isn't.

CARLA. The gun, the hut, palm fronds! *(To **WILLIAM**.)* And you! I got to school on a scholarship, worked two jobs and graduated in the top ten, but I'm having trouble figuring this out.

WILLIAM. Having a bit of trouble myself.

BARBARA. I certainly don't remember him sitting behind me in a class on Modern Literature. I'm starting to doubt we went to the same school.

CARLA. You just said you were friends in college! You said he was class clown!

BARBARA. Did I?

CARLA. *(To **WILLIAM**.)* She did, didn't she?

WILLIAM. My memory is sketchy.

CARLA. She just said it! Loony tunes, both of you!

BARBARA. Are all children from the south side impolite to their elders?

CARLA. No ma'am, just me, but I'm a reporter. Reporters don't have to be polite. They just have to be able to figure things out and get the story.

WILLIAM. When you figure this out clue me in.

CARLA. So, ok. You're trying to make my head spin and you're doing a good job. I can't prove she is who I think she is. I don't know who you are, and I'm not sure who I am anymore. But kids from the south side are stubborn. I'm going to find out.

WILLIAM. She would have shot you, you know.

CARLA. It would have been worth it. This is a big story, the AP will pick it up. But I admit I'm confused.

WILLIAM. I as well. Did she find me on the streets of New York, or did I sit behind her in Lit class? Was I an Irish lad with a song in my heart, or did I go to synagogue in the Bronx?

CARLA. She said Brooklyn!

WILLIAM. Brooklyn? I don't believe I've ever been in Brooklyn.

CARLA. Are you or aren't you William McPeak?

WILLIAM. Hard to tell. Am I a poet with my face on the back of a book cover, or a lazy son-of-a-bitch who carves his name in barroom tables? Now there's a story for you, darlin' girl. Let's work it out. What do you say? If you agree to help me solve the mystery of my identity I shall escort you down to the D&D where we'll absorb a bit of local color while sipping an icy brew.

CARLA. And let her slip away? She's good at that. I'm staying here.

WILLIAM. Come along little one. Seize the moment as the saints say. Is it the saints who say seize the moment? Well, whoever. Even if it turns out I'm not a bard I shall write you a bonny verse. Listen to me. Bonny verse. Good God, I might be a Scot! *(To* **BARBARA**.*)* Fancy that!

BARBARA. Fancy that.

WILLIAM. I might be a highlander climbing the crags with heather in my hair singing rough ballads with Bobbie Burns! *(Recites with a Scottish accent.)*
> "The king sits in Dumferling toune,
> Drinking the blude-reid wine:
> O whar will I get a guid sailor
> To sail this schip of mine?"

(He swings into a brief highland fling and laughing turns to **BARBARA**. *Her head is lowered.)* Barbara? *(No response.)* Barbara? *(No response.)* Barbara! *(Turns to* **CARLA**.*)* My basket! (**CARLA** *runs for the basket. Kneeling beside* **BARBARA** *he removes a bottle.)* A bit of rum, sweetheart? Come, love, open your eyes. *(He lifts the bottle to her lips.)* Open your lips, love. Come now, a wee bit of rum. *(Suddenly opening her eyes she pushes his hand away.)* Ah, now, *(To* **CARLA**.*)* She's come around. *(To* **BARBARA**.*)* You've given us quite a fright. Left us for a moment, you did.

BARBARA. *(Sitting upright.)* I was sleeping.

WILLIAM. Sleeping?

BARBARA. Sleeping! *(Rises, stamps her feet, moves stage left.)*

WILLIAM. Sleeping whilst I was reciting Bobbie Burns and dancin' a highland fling?

BARBARA. Sleeping while you were amusing yourself and the child. When I'm bored I nod off. *(To* **CARLA**.*)* Hand me my gun. *(***CARLA** *turns to* **WILLIAM**.*)* My shotgun! *(***WILLIAM** *nods.* **CARLA** *gives her the gun.)* I'm going to see if those bastards are back. *(Exits stage left.)*

WILLIAM. We have drug dealers hiding booty in the mangrove roots.

CARLA. Is she...

WILLIAM. She's everything you can imagine and more.

CARLA. But did she...

WILLIAM. Did she nap or did she swoon? I've no idea. All I know is that she's bloody wonderful. Bloody? Bloody wonderful? Good God, maybe I'm an Englishman! Maybe she was right. I'm a bloody Englishman out in the noonday sun!

CARLA. *(Grinning in spite of herself.)* A poet knighted by the queen?

WILLIAM. More likely an uncouth sod from down on the docks. And as such I shall nurse my inferiority with a bit of the healing balm. *(Lifts the bottle, takes a swig.)* Join me? No, bawdy bloke that I am, I'll not stoop to tempting wee ones. As an Englishman I have enough on my conscience. *(Drops the bottle back in the basket.)*

CARLA. She's not well, is she?

WILLIAM. She's lucid most of the time.

CARLA. Physically. Is she well physically?

WILLIAM. Damned if I know.

CARLA. She's not well, and you're trying to protect her.

WILLIAM. I'm trying to seduce her.

CARLA. You're protecting her from intruders.

WILLIAM. I'm not adverse to having her alone.

CARLA. If she's sick, and they say she is, she should be in the hands of a doctor.

WILLIAM. I've only operated a few times, but they were successful.

CARLA. Ok, maybe she's not sick, physically, that is. But if she is Dr. Tyler, and I'm sure she is, you don't wreck a career like her's for no reason. *(Snaps her fingers.)* She had a breakdown like they said and took off for the only home she ever had.

WILLIAM. This place?

CARLA. Your love. Am I getting close?

WILLIAM. She swears she had no idea I was here.

CARLA. And you believe her?

WILLIAM. I've never believed a word she said.

CARLA. I've worked it out, haven't I? When she shot out the windshield and ran she ran back to the boy who sat behind her in Lit class 30 years ago. The boy who saw moonbeams in her hair.

WILLIAM. She claims she came to save the Everglades.

CARLA. Sorry, you're not succeeding.

WILLIAM. Not succeeding?

CARLA. Not succeeding in confusing me anymore.

WILLIAM. And I'm the lad with the burning yearning?

CARLA. You are. I know you are.

WILLIAM. Give me a moment to convince myself.

CARLA. I can write, too. How's this? Reclusive middle-age environmentalist comes out of seclusion to give a graduation address, then exits the auditorium, blasts the windshield of her car in front of a thousand proud parents and disappears!

WILLIAM. It has a certain...

CARLA. Wait, I'm not finished... only to be found by a cub reporter sitting in a rocking chair in the sub-tropics with a shotgun across her knees imagining she's saving the Everglades!

WILLIAM. Does anyone really care.

CARLA. You bet they care! She's a second Rachel Carson! Writes like an angel and fights like a devil for privacy. Photographers stalked her for a picture of that face! And she wouldn't have done what she did unless she was sick.

WILLIAM. I've done worse in the best of health.

CARLA. She ran to the arms of the man who never stopped loving her.

WILLIAM. To the arms of this aged fellow?

CARLA. You're not old.

WILLIAM. Oh, darlin' girl, old I am. More's the pity. Look at these hands. Old and dented they are, dented by a hard life without love.

CARLA. Poets are ageless. *(She turns to* **BARBARA**, *who has entered stage left.)* Poets are ageless, aren't they?

BARBARA. The old dog does have ageless enthusiasm.

WILLIAM. Interlopers gone?

BARBARA. Gone, drat 'em. I had hoped to pepper their rumps with gunshot.

WILLIAM. Fie on Barbarry Allan. *(Begins to slowly dance, singing the first few lines of the Irish folk song, Barbarry Allan.)*

"I fell in love with a nice young girl,

Her name was Barbarry Allan,

I fell in love with a nice young girl,

Her name was Barbarry Allan.

(He draws **BARBARA** *into his arms and they dance together as he sings.)*

Till I fell sick and was very ill,

I sent for Barbarry Allen,

Till I feel sick and was very ill,

I sent for Barbarry Allen.

(He lowers **BARBARA** *into the rocker, turns to* **CARLA**.*)* Off key and a croaky voice, but I'm a man who loves to sing.

CARLA. You're no Pavarotti, but you're an OK poet. "Cooling his toes in the mouth of his consort, his lovely consort, Parvati." Gives me shivers.

WILLIAM. My lady tells me I didn't write that poem, nonetheless may I take a bow? *(Deep bow.)* Oops, sometimes it happens when I bend over.

CARLA. What?

WILLIAM. I fart.

CARLA. Alright, have fun. Would you rather I'd said it was piss awful?

WILLIAM. Perhaps it is.

CARLA. Oh, sweet Mother Mary, I've been a fool! *(Repeats the line from the song, Barbarry Allen.)* "Till I fell sick and was very ill!" *(Spins around to face **BARBARA**.)* He's the one who's ill! He's not taking care of you, you're taking care of him! The boy with the song in his heart!

WILLIAM. A bit of the blarney, as my saintly mother used to say.

CARLA. Was the poem we read in class the last song you sang before she blind-sided you?

WILLIAM. Blind-sided me?

CARLA. *(To **BARBARA**.)* Because you took off, didn't you? You had a diploma from Harvard to hang on a wall. You weren't content to be some man's muse. You had books to write and seminars to teach and an illusive face the press found fascinating. *(Mimes clicking a camera.)* The seclusive Dr. Tyler leaving the lecture hall!

WILLIAM. I still find that face fascinating.

CARLA. *(To **WILLIAM**.)* And you found fame, too, didn't you? Books of poetry with your picture on the cover. But the beer was flat and the wine bitter after she took off, and you found yourself roaming the back streets of big cities at night stepping over puddles of urine searching for your lovely Parvati…

WILLIAM. *(Mimes writing.)* Slower, please, I'm taking notes…

CARLA. *(Ignoring him.)* Finally hiding away on a mosquito infested island drinking yourself to death.

WILLIAM. *(Mimes writing.)* Down the tube with demon rum. *(Stops.)* Haven't I heard of someone who…. Mon Dieu, I'm French! From the south of France! *(Assumes a French accent.)* Following in the footsteps of that wastrel, Gauguin, and going to pot on a tropical isle!

CARLA. Can I continue?

BARBARA. May I continue. Proper grammar.

CARLA. Screw proper grammar!

WILLIAM. Tut tut.

CARLA. So the lady intellectual with deep pockets and a full set of the Encyclopedia Britannica gets wind that the boy with the song in his heart is a permanent fixture at the local bar on some island forsaken by the good Lord and junks her career to save him.

(WILLIAM and BARBARA laugh.)

CARLA. OK, laugh. But see who laughs last.

WILLIAM. Oh, darlin' girl, we're not laughing at you. Come closer and I'll tell you a secret.

CARLA. *(Not moving.)* What?

WILLIAM. We're afraid of you.

CARLA. Yeah, right. *(Turns to BARBARA.)* You, too? *(BARBARA nods.)* Afraid of someone you call a child?

BARBARA. Children can't keep secrets.

CARLA. And kids from the projects are dangerous, too. When we get our teeth into something we shake it until…

BARBARA. Until?

CARLA. Until it gives up.

BARBARA. And if it refuses to give up?

CARLA. We leave it in a heap on the sidewalk. So I ask again. Are you Dr. Barbara Tyler?

WILLIAM. From where I sit she's a helluva good likeness or a helluva good actress.

CARLA. And are you William McPeak?

BARBARA. He's trod the boards. He's an excellent actor. *(WILLIAM bows.)* And a play just closed in Sarasota.

WILLIAM. *(Spreading his arms.)* Out of work actors soaking up the sun.

CARLA. That sauce won't sell. But I'll tell you what will.

WILLIAM. What's that?

CARLA. The truth!

WILLIAM. Who's truth? Some say truth is a prism. Most of us seeing but one facet.

BARBARA. And what right have you to know the truth? You barge in here uninvited and demand to know the truth?

CARLA. Can't wait to pepper my rump with gunshot, can you?

BARBARA. I've got the itch.

CARLA. Well, so have I! I'm itching to see your face splashed across the front page! I'm itching to read the story with my name in the by-line!

BARBARA. Leave now!

CARLA. You have a choice you snotty white Anglo-Saxon tree hugger! Tell me what's going on, or I'll compose my own version in purple prose!

BARBARA. You have a choice, you unprincipled Neopolitan new hound! Get out or... *(Raises the gun.)*

CARLA. Too good to say, "beat it, bitch?"

BARBARA. *(Aims the gun at* **CARLA.***)* Beat it, bi... *(Checks herself.)* Last chance.

CARLA. *(Leaps forward, grabs the gun and throws it to the ground.)* Think again!

(Fists clenched, **BARBARA** *starts to rise, drops back, closes her eyes, rocks furiously* **CARLA** *jambs her foot on the rocker.)*

None of that shit!

BARBARA. You have a mouth on you!

CARLA. I've never talked like this to anyone before! My nana would wash my mouth! You bring out the worst in me!

(Silence.)

BARBARA. *(Wearily.)* It's hard not to like you. But I'll manage.

CARLA. I have to hand in something. You want reporters tramping through your spatterdock and white water lilies? You want some snot-nosed kid like me asking to see a license for that gun?

WILLIAM. Is she wearing you out, love?

BARBARA. It's alright, Will. *(To* **CARLA.***)* I can't stop you, can I?

CARLA. No.

BARBARA. You can taste it, can't you?

CARLA. Taste what?

BARBARA. Whatever it is you're determined to have.

CARLA. I'm determined to have this story.

BARBARA. That's the beginning. What's the end?

CARLA. I don't know.

BARBARA. We seldom do until we find we find ourselves there and count the cost.

CARLA. I'll worry about that later.

BARBARA. Yes, you will.

CARLA. Look, the sooner you answer some questions the sooner you'll see my rear end. Not peppered with gunshot, I hope. So tell me, Dr. Barbara Tyler, why did you disappear? They say you were sick. Were you sick?

BARBARA. Was I sick? Yes, I suppose I was sick.

CARLA. So you high-tailed it down here.

BARBARA. So I high-tailed it down here.

CARLA. Why?

BARBARA. Because while I was toasting my toes in a Fifth Avenue apartment waiting for those who read what I wrote to save the wetlands half the Everglades disappeared.

WILLIAM. And now this lovely lunatic is trying to save a patch of Eden herself.

CARLA. This is Eden?

WILLIAM. Is to her.

CARLA. And you?

WILLIAM. Adam got to hang out with Eve.

BARBARA. How did you know I was here?

CARLA. Read you books. You're hooked on those Indians.

WILLIAM. The Calusa.

BARBARA. A highly civilized people.

CARLA. Whatever. And they hung out down here.

WILLIAM. More than a thousand years ago.

CARLA. So, OK. More than a thousand years ago. Figured this was my best bet. I've been sloshing around for weeks doing the Sherlock thing.

BARBARA. With no regard for privacy.

CARLA. You can't prance in front of cameras for a decade then demand privacy. You can't call this Eden, dig a moat and blast all comers.

BARBARA. A strange Eden, yes, but an Eden for the hunted, the destitute, the dispossessed, the world weary.

CARLA. If I remember the story when old Eve bit the apple and lied about it she was booted out. And since I want to see my name in the Sunday Times, sorry, but you're going to feel my toe on your butt.

BARBARA. You're saying I lie?

CARLA. Like a pro.

BARBARA. If I've lied it's been to myself.

CARLA. No, you lied to me about who you are.

BARBARA. I don't know who I am.

CARLA. You're Dr. Barbara Tyler.

BARBARA. That's who I was.

CARLA. I'm up to here with word games! And if this is Eden, Eden's a bore! What do you do for excitement?

BARBARA. Mornings I weave baskets of palm fronds and make mats for my floor.

WILLIAM. And lets the old shot gun rip now and then just for the hell of it.

(**BARBARA** *raises the shot gun and pulls the trigger.*)

CARLA. (*Jumps as the shot rings out.*) Oh, my God! (**WILLIAM** *slaps his knee, laughing with delight.*) That's not funny. She might hit something!

WILLIAM. Depends on the time of day. After her nap her aim is deplorable. Before noon she hits nine out of ten. *(Pulls up his trouser leg to reveal a large bandage.)*

CARLA. She shot you?

WILLIAM. Before noon she rarely misses.

BARBARA. He scratches his mosquito bites.

WILLIAM. Is that why I'm limping? *(Whispers to CARLA.)* I shall be more careful when I bow this time. *(A deep bow to BARBARA.)* I apologize.

CARLA. I don't get it. If people tripped over each other to buy a book I wrote I'd stash my nana in a splashy apartment, buy first class tickets to Rome, wheel her through the Vatican and maybe get an audience with the Pope!

(Silence.)

WILLIAM. *(Moves to BARBARA, lifts her hand. To CARLA.)* What do you see?

CARLA. A hand.

WILLIAM. The hand of a young woman?

CARLA. No.

WILLIAM. No. The hand of a woman who sits on a silken sofa nibbling fine chocolate?

CARLA. No.

WILLIAM. No. You're looking at the hand of a woman who worked tirelessly.

CARLA. And filled auditoriums!

WILLIAM. And sat alone when applause died and auditoriums emptied.

CARLA. Should have gone out and had a drink!

BARBARA. Where?

CARLA. Anywhere!

WILLIAM. Anywhere is nowhere. Ask a fellow who downed drinks in seedy bars on five continents.

CARLA. And now she's sitting alone out here!

BARBARA. Oh, child, I'm not alone. *(Rises, moves downstage and looks out over what is water.)* When the sun sets over the Gulf I see the shadows of amber-skin men bringing in the day's catch. I see the shadows of women crouching by cooking fires. I hear the high, sweet voices of children at play and the tinkle of shell necklaces. And when I lie on my cot at night I dream their dreams.

WILLIAM. *(Moves behind* **BARBARA**, *wraps his arms around her.)* And wakes in the morning to eat papaya and let the juice run down her chin. And sits again at sunset to watch the clouds flame and burn. *(She turns, rests her head on his shoulder.)* Weary? *(She nods. He leads her gently to the rocker.)*

CARLA. *(After a moment.)* And when the story breaks, hordes of reporters, right?

WILLIAM. Right.

CARLA. I'm tough. Had to be to make my way. But look, my nana has a room to let. You can hide out with her when the story breaks. House smells of marinara sauce, but you'll have your privacy. No one gets past my nana. She's ferocious.

WILLIAM. No match for you, little one.

CARLA. I need the tape. And I need my camera. If I don't get them I'll blow your cover as soon as I find a phone.

WILLIAM. *(Massaging* **BARBARA***'s shoulders.)* Is she wearing you out, love? *(To* **CARLA**.*)* You're wearing her out.

CARLA. If I have to wear her out to get the story that's what I'll do.

WILLIAM. I don't think so.

CARLA. You going to stop me?

WILLIAM. I may or may not be a poet, but I'm certainly not a perfect gentleman. I've been known to spank a child.

CARLA. And I've been slapped around a lot, but it hasn't stopped me. *(To* **BARBARA**.*)* You're a fighter! This place isn't my idea of Eden, but I like trees and flowers and stuff. Some of us got sent to the country when we were kids, and I still remember the smell of cut grass. I even like dandelions. Who's going to make sure there'll be dandelions in everyone's front lawn if you sit here weaving baskets out of palm fronds?

BARBARA. I appoint you keeper of the dandelions.

CARLA. Me?

BARBARA. You.

CARLA. Yeah, sure. *(To* **WILLIAM.***)* And what's a world without poetry, William McPeak?

WILLIAM. Dreary. Write a verse.

CARLA. Me?

WILLIAM. You.

CARLA. And when do I run for president? Why me? *(Circles the stage.)* I'm a good girl. I cuss, but I still go to confession! Why me?

WILLIAM. Darlin' girl?

CARLA. What?

WILLIAM. When you get to the Vatican you could tell the good brothers you blessed this woman with time to heal.

CARLA. Damn you! *(Sinks to the ground, pounds her fist in the dirt.)* Damn you! *(Sniffles, wipes her eyes with her fist smearing dirt on her cheek.)* I hate you! I hate you both! This is my big chance! *(Removes her shoe, studies her toes.)* I'm going to get a fungus!

WILLIAM. *(As* **CARLA** *puts her shoe back on he takes the thermos from his basket, wets his kerchief, raises her to her feet and wipes her face.)* There, that's better. You're really very pretty.

CARLA. *(Breaks away, stamps stage right, spins around.)* So I have to write a poem, save the environment and win an election for president!

WILLIAM. You have my vote.

CARLA. And when do I get to be Pope? *(Sticks out her tongue, lifts the knapsack, starts to leave.)*

BARBARA. Carla? *(***CARLA** *turns. She picks up the recorder and camera, holds them out.)*

CARLA. *(Turns to* **WILLIAM.** *He nods. She moves slowly back to*

COSTUME PLOT

BARBARA wears khaki trousers, colorful cotton shirt and waterproof boots.

CARLA wears a white t-shirt, dark trousers and sneakers.

WILLIAM wears worn jeans, red sweatshirt, yellow kerchief and waterproof boots.

PROPERTY PLOT

Properties brought on stage by a character:

BARBARA sits on stage with a shotgun in her lap.

CARLA carries a backpack containing a small camera and tape recorder with a newspaper clipping, pad and pen in her pocket.

WILLIAM carries an old basket containing a few flowers, a thermos and a small bottle of liquor. In his pocket he carries a ring.

SET PLOT

The stage is bare except for an old rocking chair and a stool. Edging stage right are large cutouts of wild bushes of various heights and shades of green.

BARBARA, *takes the offered items.)* Thank you. *(Moves stage right, hesitates, turns, runs back to* **BARBARA** *and drops them in her lap.)*

BARBARA. *(Softly.)* Thank you.

CARLA. Yeah. *(Starts to exit, turns.)* But remember, I have perfect memory! *(Exits stage right.)*

WILLIAM. Helluva kid. *(Moves stage right, stares at the departing figure, turns.)* Is it time?

BARBARA. Yes, Will, past time. Oh! *(Her hands fly to her face.)* I'm a mess. *(Her hands fly to her hair.)* And my hair!

WILLIAM. *(Withdraws her hands from her hair, kisses them.)* Oh, my dear, I see moonbeams in you hair in mid-morning. Barbara Tyler, or whoever you are, will you marry me… again? *(She extends her left hand. He draws a ring from his pocket, polishes it with his kerchief, slips it on her ring finger.)*

BARBARA. I've missed it.

WILLIAM. *(Lowers himself on the stool. They sit quietly a moment holding hands.)* Her nana probably makes a helluva sauce. If she writes the story shall we hang out in the room the old gal is renting, brew dandelion wine in the cellar? On the other hand we could head for Israel and hide in those caves above the Dead Sea. You could bob in the salt water below and grow fat and rosy while I finish the Dead Sea Scrolls in verse.

CARLA. *(Appears stage right scratching her arm.)* Just remembered, alligators and cottonmouth snakes! I don't want to be walking in circles again. How about pointing the way out of here.

WILLIAM. I'll lead the way, darlin' girl.

CARLA. Thanks. *(Exits, pops back.)* And by the way, I'm not Italian! *(She's gone.)*

WILLIAM. *(Laughing, slaps his knee.)* Fooled me! *(Walks stage left, turns, winks at* **BARBARA**, *exits.)*

*(***BARBARA** *leans back smiling, closes her eyes and rocks.)*

End of the play

ONE WHITE WINTER NIGHT

A PLAY IN ONE ACT

CAST OF CHARACTERS

MARTHA – A woman in her early forties dressed severely in a black dress, her hair pulled back in a bun.

JUNE – Her younger sister whose hair curls softly around a pretty face. She wears a pink dress with full skirt.

VIOLET – Their sixteen year old niece who is confined to a wheel chair. She wears an ethereal white dress, her long hair pulled back with a lavender ribbon.

RODNEY – An amiable middle-age traveling salesman dressed in light blue suit and flowered tie.

SCENE

The action takes place on a front porch in a small town.

TIME

The year nineteen hundred and forty nine.

At Rise. *Two old fashioned white rocking chairs sit stage center. They are the type of rocking chairs once seen on wide front porches facing small town sidewalks where couples sat in the evening greeting neighbors strolling past. Downstage right and left are large containers brimming with pink roses and purple petunias.*

As the play opens **JUNE** *enters up stage left followed by* **MARTHA** *who pushes* **VIOLET** *in a small wheel chair.* **VIOLET** *carries a doll with porcelain face. Until the end of the play she speaks and sings softly only to mama and her dolly.*

JUNE *seats herself in rocker stage right,* **MARTHA** *to her left with the wheel chair beside her. The two older women simultaneously sigh, lean back, close their eyes and begin to rock.*

JUNE. *(After a moment.)* Lovely day.
MARTHA. Lovely.

(Brief silence.)

JUNE. *(Opens her eyes, glances at* **VIOLET***, crosses to the young woman)* Isn't it heavenly to sit here in the sun? Shall we rock, sweetheart?
MARTHA. Yes, dear, Auntie June will start you rocking.

*(***JUNE*** rocks the chair gently a moment, kisses* **VIOLET** *on the head , returns to her chair. She and* **MARTHA** *sigh, lean back, close their eyes and rock.)*

JUNE. Lovely day.
MARTHA. Lovely.
JUNE. The sun is so…
MARTHA. So warm…
JUNE. On my shoulders…
MARTHA. On my knees.

JUNE. Violet, dear, isn't it lovely to sit on the porch in the summer sun?

(VIOLET turns to stare at them. After a moment she cuddles dolly and smiles sweetly. The two older women give each other a satisfied glance, lean back, close their eyes and rock.)

MARTHA. Days of rain. Dreadful.

JUNE. Rain is good for the garden.

(Rock a moment without speaking.)

MARTHA. Good for your garden, yes.

JUNE. How are your knees?

MARTHA. Bless the Lord, my knees...

JUNE. Did you take your pills?

MARTHA. *(Her eyes pop open.)* Of course I took my pills!

JUNE. *(Sensing a spat she opens her eyes and says soothingly.)* Sister, you're a saint. I feel so guilty being the picture of health. *(Giggles.)* Rodney says I'm the picture of health, not only pretty, but peppy.

MARTHA. You're a picture of health as that man says, because you take life lightly. You take life lightly don't you, June?

JUNE. I have the sense not to worry.

MARTHA. You've left the worrying to me.

JUNE. *(Lightly.)* Because you're so good at it.

MARTHA. You wouldn't have milk on your cereal if not for me.

JUNE. That's true, Martha, that's true.

MARTHA. No butter on the plate, nothing in the cupboard but for me.

JUNE. That's true.

MARTHA. Indeed.

VIOLET. *(To dolly in a soft singsong voice.)* But for me...

MARTHA. *(To* **VIOLET.***)* No, dear, but for me.

VIOLET. *(To dolly.)* No, dear, but for me...

MARTHA. *(Sighing.)* Yes, dear, but for you.

VIOLET. *(Rocking dolly.)* But for you…

>   (**MARTHA** *glances at* **JUNE**. *They shake their heads sadly, lean back and close their eyes. Silence.*)

JUNE. *(After a moment rises, plucks a flower from a container, tucks it in her bodice, twirls, skips across the stage, lifts* **VIOLET***'s face and kiss her on the nose.)* You've been blessed to be so beautiful, sweetheart, and I've been blessed with sturdy knees.

MARTHA. Because you're not behind a counter all day. *(To* **VIOLET***.)* It's because your Aunt June doesn't spend the day behind a counter.

JUNE. That's true, Martha. You're so good to us. And I'm so foolish. It's just that it's such a beautiful day. And when I'm on the dance floor I'm a girl again. Rodney says when I'm on the dance floor I'm a girl again. *(Twirls then sinks back in her chair laughing.)*

>   *(A moment's silence.)*

MARTHA. He has thin ankles.

JUNE. Who?

MARTHA. Mr. Egan. His trouser legs aren't long enough. One glimpses his ankles.

JUNE. He's a fine looking man for his age.

MARTHA. Mother said that a gentleman friend, if one has a gentleman friend, should wear trousers of a proper length.

JUNE. I never heard mother say such a thing.

MARTHA. Never once did I glimpse our father's ankles.

JUNE. Papa was a bit old fashioned. Papa never wore a bathing suit.

VIOLET. *(Singing to dolly.)* Never wore a…

MARTHA. *(To* **VIOLET***.)* It seems your Aunt June has a gentleman friend.

VIOLET. *(Singing to dolly.)* Gentleman friend… gentleman friend. St. Peter dolly's gentleman friend…

MARTHA. Hush! You mustn't say such things! St. Peter is not dolly's gentleman friend!

(Cringing at MARTHA's vehemence VIOLET lets dolly drop to the floor.)

JUNE. Martha! *(Rushes to VIOLET, picks up dolly.)* Certainly St. Peter is dolly's... dolly's gentleman friend! *(Tucks dolly in VIOLET's arm.)*

MARTHA. You manage to fill that child's head with foolishness.

JUNE. We've been reading Bible stories from the book you bought her.

MARTHA. No more books! No more books!

VIOLET. *(Sadly to dolly.)* No more...

MARTHA. *(Takes an embroidered handkerchief from her pocket, dabs her forehead, sinks back, closes her eyes. After a moment.)* He's fat.

VIOLET. St. Peter is...

MARTHA. *(Bolts upright.)* No, no, not St. Peter! Your aunt's gentleman friend! *(To JUNE.)* He's fat!

JUNE. A little overweight.

MARTHA. Fat!

JUNE. Fat men are light on their feet! And he loves to dance!

VIOLET. *(Whispers to dolly.)* St. Peter loves to...

MARTHA. *(To VIOLET.)* Don't listen to a word Aunt June says! Your Aunt June is a foolish woman!

(VIOLET slumps in her chair.)

JUNE. *(Crosses behind MARTHA, whispers.)* Shame on you! *(Gently rocking VIOLET's chair.)* Aunt Martha is right, sweetheart. I'm a foolish woman. I don't know that the good saints dance, but I'm sure they're fond of music. Why in heaven your mama, our dear sister, listens to angels playing on their harps. *(She plucks a flower from one of the containers and tucks it in VIOLET's blouse.)*

(A silence.)

MARTHA. And he giggles.

JUNE. What?

MARTHA. He giggles. I suspect a man who giggles. When I wait on a man who giggles I count the money twice. "Oh," such a man will say, "I thought I gave you a twenty." Does he over tip?

JUNE. I never noticed.

MARTHA. Well notice. Fat men who giggle take advantage of women like you.

JUNE. Women like me?

MARTHA. Women who blow out more then 40 candles on their birthday cake and announce they're changing their name. I shall not call you Rosalie. *(To* **VIOLET.***)* We shall not call Aunt June Rosalie.

JUNE. I'm a flower, Rodney says. I'm as lovely and as fragrant as a flower.

MARTHA. Because you sprinkle mother's eau de cologne on your bodice. You were christened June and June you are. *(To* **VIOLET.***)* You are the flower of this family, dear.

JUNE. *(Rushing to* **VIOLET.***)* Yes, sweetheart, you are the flower of this family. *(Whispers.)* But you can call me Rosalie. We'll be two little flowers in the garden. *(She does a dance step, twirls, skips downstage to look up and down the sidewalk.)* He'll be along soon.

VIOLET. Call me Rosalie…

MARTHA. No, dear, you're Violet, I'm Aunt Martha, she's Rosalie. *(***JUNE** *whirls around and claps with delight.)* No, no, she's June! *(To* **JUNE.***)* You're impossible. *(Distraught.)* My knees ache.

JUNE. Sister, dear.

MARTHA. And my feet. On my feet all day.

JUNE. You're so good to us.

MARTHA. I do my best. *(To* **VIOLET.***)* I once had a gentleman friend.

JUNE. *(To* **VIOLET.***)* Yes, Aunt Martha once had a gentleman friend.

MARTHA. Indeed.

JUNE. *(Again scans the sidewalk, turns to* **VIOLET.***)* Rodney is taking me dancing.

MARTHA. Violet shall call him Mr. Egan.

JUNE. *(Swaying, she sings.)* We've rings on our fingers and bells on our toes…

(Pause.)

MARTHA. Dinner.

JUNE. What?

MARTHA. What shall we have for dinner?

JUNE. Rodney is taking me out to eat.

MARTHA. Violet and I. We have to eat, too.

JUNE. Of course.

MARTHA. *(After a moment.)* Fish.

JUNE. Fish?

MARTHA. Tuna fish salad.

JUNE. You're tuna fish salad is tasty.

MARTHA. I don't thin the mayonnaise. Mother, God rest her soul, thinned the mayonnaise.

JUNE. Rest her soul, she did.

(They chuckle.)

MARTHA. Revenge.

JUNE. Revenge?

MARTHA. On Father. She had little ways of taking revenge on father.

JUNE. For sitting in his chair Sunday mornings.

MARTHA. She curled our hair with the curling iron, dabbed Vaseline on our patent leather shoes so they would shine and off to church we'd go while he sat glued to his chair reading the Sunday paper.

JUNE. But mama loved him.

MARTHA. Of course she loved him, but she had her revenge. We all have our little revenge. Mama thinned the mayonnaise.

JUNE. *(Twirling.)* Mama thinned the mayonnaise… *(Dances across to* **VIOLET**.*)* Remember, sweetheart, how your mama would dip a spoon into the jar of mayonnaise and let you lick it?

MARTHA. How can she remember? She was only two when the…

JUNE. Of course she remembers. *(To **VIOLET**.)* Cool thick mayonnaise on your tongue? *(Moves behind **MARTHA**'s chair, messages her sister's forehead while singing softly.)* Cool thick mayonnaise on her baby's tongue.

MARTHA. *(Breathing deeply.)* Ah…

JUNE. Relax, sister, dear, relax…

MARTHA. Yes… *(Sinks back in her chair.)* Yes… *(Seems to drift off to sleep.)*

*(**JUNE**, messaging **MARTHA**'s forehead, senses her sister is dozing, tip-toes to her own chair, sits in rocker smiling.)*

VIOLET. *(Very softly.)* Mama?

MARTHA. *(Wakens.)* What is it, dear?

VIOLET. *(Rocking dolly.)* Dolly wants mama…

MARTHA. Tell dolly to hush. Your mother is in heaven.

VIOLET. *(As if telling dolly.)* Mama in heaven… Mayonnaise in heaven…

MARTHA. No, no. There is mayonnaise in the refrigerator. Now lean back and close your eyes. You didn't sleep well last night.

JUNE. How can she sleep with you walking the floor?

MARTHA. I walk the floor wondering how I'll pay for the upkeep of this house and feed two children!

JUNE. Two children?

MARTHA. Two children! You're a child as well as Violet, a pampered child who powders her nose and romances a man with thin ankles.

VIOLET. Mayonnaise in heaven with mama…

MARTHA. *(To **VIOLET**.)* Stop that foolishness.

JUNE. Martha! *(Rushes to **VIOLET**'s chair.)* We do miss mama, don't we? Of course we do. Mama dipped a teaspoon into the jar of mayonnaise and let you lick it, didn't she? Aunt Martha was teasing, sweetheart. *(To **MARTHA**.)* You were teasing, weren't you?

MARTHA. *(Stiffly.)* Yes. Of course. I was teasing.

JUNE. *(To* **VIOLET**.*)* The sun has warmed the freckles on your dear little nose.

MARTHA. Violet does not have freckles.

JUNE. Indeed she does. *(Counting.)* One, two, three. *(To* **VIOLET**.*)* You have three freckles on your dear little nose. *(Kisses* **VIOLET**, *turns to* **MARTHA**.*)* You've saddened the child.

MARTHA. It's my nerves. I'm ashamed.

JUNE. Oh, sister, it's I who should be ashamed. You work so hard, and I'm quite useless. I have no talent.

MARTHA. You have a talent for happiness. I hear you singing in the kitchen.

JUNE. While you walk the floor at night. Perhaps I should….

MARTHA. Should what?

JUNE. Move in with Aunt Alva.

MARTHA. Move in with Aunt Alva? You'll do no such thing.

JUNE. Violet and I.

MARTHA. And leave me here alone? Who would make me laugh? Who would tend the roses? Who would fill the house with flowers as our mother did?

JUNE. It isn't difficult to arrange a bouquet.

MARTHA. I haven't a green thumb.

JUNE. Oh, sister, I'm a burden.

MARTHA. You'll stay right here. Forgive me. Will I ever learn to hold my tongue?

JUNE. No, forgive me for singing in the kitchen. For waking you when you've finally gotten to sleep. You're the bulwark of this family. *(To* **VIOLET**.*)* Aunt Martha is the bulwark of this family, isn't she? And look, she has freckles, too. Yes, you do, Martha. Let me count them, one, two, three…

MARTHA. *(Grasps her hand.)* If you left me, June, who would make me laugh? Without you in the house I'm afraid I'd thin the mayonnaise.

JUNE. Then, of course, I must stay. *(Returns to her rocker.)*

VIOLET. *(Singing to dolly.)* Afraid I'd thin the mayonnaise….

MARTHA. No, no, dear. As long as you're in the house I shan't thin the mayonnaise.

(The two older women smile. They close their eyes, lean back and rock. **RODNEY** *enters down stage right on what is the sidewalk, jingling coins in his pocket. He stops, straightens his tie, bends to brush dust from his shoes with his handkerchief, takes a breath sweetener from his pocket and sprays his mouth.)*

JUNE. Lovely day.

MARTHA. Lovely.

(Seeing the sisters sitting on the porch **RODNEY** *smooths his hair, pulls in his stomach and mimes climbing the porch steps.)*

RODNEY. Bon jour, lovely ladies.

JUNE. *(Clapping her hands with delight.)* Gracious, Rodney, you caught us napping.

MARTHA. Bon jour?

JUNE. French. French for hello. Isn't he clever? *(Holds out her hand.)* Bon jour, Rodney.

RODNEY. *(Lifts her hand, kisses it.)* Ma petite Cherie.

VIOLET. *(Rocking dolly.)* Cherie… Cherie…

MARTHA. We speak English in this house, Mr. Egan. *(To* **VIOLET.**) We speak English, dear.

JUNE. Rodney spent time in Paris.

RODNEY. The Paris of artists and street cafes. You would be the toast of Paris, little Rosalie, wealthy men would court you, starving artists paint you, designers beg you to wear their frocks.

JUNE. *(To* **MARTHA.**) He's such a tease.

MARTHA. Indeed.

RODNEY. *(Bowing to* **JUNE.**) May I be your escort tonight?

JUNE. *(Playing along.)* I had invitations, of course, from wealthy men and starving artists, but I'd rather spend the evening with you.

RODNEY. Shall we go dancing?

JUNE. Let's do.

RODNEY. And have a bit of the bubbly?

JUNE. A bit of the bubbly, yes.

MARTHA. A bit of the bubbly?

RODNEY. Champagne, dear lady.

MARTHA. There has never been a drop of alcohol in this house.

JUNE. My sister is a bit old-fashioned.

MARTHA. Your sister is an upright woman.

RODNEY. Rosalie likes a bit of fun.

MARTHA. Her name is June.

RODNEY. Yes, dear lady. June likes a bit of fun. *(Winks at **JUNE**.)*

JUNE. Rodney is teaching me to dip.

MARTHA. Dip?

*(**RODNEY** assumes a pose. **JUNE** floats into his arms. They twirl, spin across the floor, he lowers her into a deep dramatic dip.)*

MARTHA. That's naughty. *(To **VIOLET**, who watches entranced.)* Don't watch your Aunt June, she is being naughty.

RODNEY. If you'd rather we didn't, dear lady.

MARTHA. Didn't?

RODNEY. Didn't dance. If you object.

MARTHA. I don't object to a waltz. Father waltzed with mother at a black tie affair, a clean white handkerchief over the hand which touched our dear mother's bare back.

JUNE. *(Clapping her hands.)* And on their anniversary. Mama would put on her ball gown and Papa would turn on the phonograph and they would dance in the parlor. Mama loved to dance.

MARTHA. With her husband. I myself waltzed when I was young.

JUNE. *(Teasing.)* Martha had a beau. You had a beau, didn't you, Martha?

MARTHA. An upright young man.

VIOLET. *(Explaining to dolly.)* Upright young man…

MARTHA. *(To **VIOLET**.)* But we don't talk about that.

VIOLET. *(To dolly.)* Don't talk…

MARTHA. Hush!

VIOLET. *(Shaking dolly.)* Hush!

JUNE. *(Moves quickly behind **MARTHA**'s chair, wraps her arms around her sister.)* I'm sorry, I do rattle on.

MARTHA. Mother often mentioned how you do rattle on! *(After a moment.)* Perhaps I'm an old silly.

VIOLET. *(Scolding dolly.)* Silly…

MARTHA. *(To **RODNEY**.)* It's true, I am a bit old fashioned. But these stiff old legs once danced till ten.

RODNEY. *(Moves to **MARTHA**, bows.)* May I have this dance, dear lady?

MARTHA. Mercy, me.

RODNEY. I'd be honored.

JUNE. Do dance, sister.

MARTHA. I'd feel a fool.

RODNEY. A few steps. Perhaps your sister will sing.

JUNE. *(Begins to sway, singing the Rodgers and Hart melody.)*
> "Blue moon, you saw me standing alone
>> without a dream in my heart
>> without a love of my own."

*(**RODNEY** holds out his hand. **MARTHA** hesitates. He helps her to her feet, they begin to dance as **JUNE** sings.)*
> "Blue moon, you saw me standing alone
>> without a dream in my heart
>> without a love of my own"

VIOLET. *(Rocking and singing softly.)* Love of my own…

*(**RODNEY** and **JUNE** sing as **MARTHA** begins to dance more easily.)*
> "Blue moon, you saw me standing alone
>> without a dream in my heart,
>> without a love of my own."

MARTHA. *(Breathless.)* Mercy me.

RODNEY. *(Lowers her gently into her chair, bows.)* Thank you, dear lady. You danced beautifully. She danced beautifully, didn't she, Rosalie?

JUNE. Martha is light on her feet.

RODNEY. A mere zephyr.

MARTHA. I once enjoyed dancing. When I was young, that is.

RODNEY. I'm sure you were a bell of the ball.

MARTHA. My dance card was always full.

RODNEY. I would have written my name.

MARTHA. Be on your way, you two.

JUNE. We won't be late.

RODNEY. *(To MARTHA and VIOLET.)* Good evening, lovely ladies.

(RODNEY and JUNE move stage right.)

MARTHA. Oh, and… not too much bubbly!

RODNEY. Trust me, dear lady.

(Smiling, they wave, exit stage right.)

MARTHA. *(Rocks a moment, turns to VIOLET.)* Our mother did not approve of alcohol so suffice it to say I have never lifted a glass of champagne to my lips. That is not to say I wasn't tempted when attending cotillions. Many a young man tempted me with a glass. You wouldn't have recognized me, dear. I wore a pale blue gown with sweetheart neck and a bow in the back. If my prayers are answered some day I'll slip it over your head and tie that bow. When your dear little mind has healed and you talk to us again. *(Rises, walks stage right, bends to sniff the roses.)* Old fashioned roses have more scent than newer ones. *(Circling the stage.)* Look at me. I'm walking like a girl again. Dancing has limbered my legs. *(Turns to VIOLET.)* Oh, Violet, but for that… for that accident!

VIOLET. *(A silence. VIOLET starts to shake.)* BOOM!

MARTHA. Dear Lord, what have I done? *(Rushes to VIOLET.)*

No, no! We mustn't think of that! *(Chaffing* **VIOLET***'s hands.)* You can't possibly remember. You were too young.

VIOLET. *(Sobs without sound.)* Mama...

MARTHA. Your mama is in heaven with the angels where we'll all be together again someday. *(Takes out her hankie and wipes* **VIOLET***'s tears.)* My, isn't it getting chilly. See how the lowering sun sets the maple leafs afire? Come, lets go in. A cup of peppermint tea will warm us. And perhaps a biscuit. *(Pushing the wheel chair stage left.)* Perhaps several. *(They exit stage left.)*

(Lights dim.. Blue Moon played softly indicates the passage of time. **JUNE** *and* **RODNEY** *enter stage right, she clinging to his arm. He kisses her lightly. She pulls away.)*

JUNE. *(Whispers.)* Martha might be watching.

RODNEY. Watching?

JUNE. From the window as mother used to do.

RODNEY. Martha is not your mother.

JUNE. But she mothers me. *(Kisses her finger, presses it to his lips.)* She is, of course, quite a bit older than I am.

RODNEY. You, my dear, are younger than springtime.

JUNE. Isn't that a song?

RODNEY. If it is I must have written it. About tomorrow.

JUNE. I'm so excited.

RODNEY. Ah, Rosalie, I'm afraid I cannot...

JUNE. But we must!

RODNEY. I fear my funds are still...

JUNE. Tied up?

RODNEY. I'm afraid so. I had expected...

JUNE. I'll take a bit more from the old cookie jar.

RODNEY. If she should count it.

JUNE. She never counts it. And I'm allowed to take a bit now and then.

RODNEY. A bit, yes, but if she should count it before my funds...

JUNE. She won't.

RODNEY. But if she does.

JUNE. If she does I'll...

RODNEY. Your sister is, as she says, an upright woman. I shouldn't want her to disapprove of me any more than she does.

JUNE. Perhaps she doesn't disapprove of you now. Not after having danced with you. The poor dear hasn't had a man's arms around her since... *(Giggles softly.)* Perhaps not even when she was being courted, for Martha believed her beau was an upright young man. As if any man excepting papa, of course, was purely upright.

RODNEY. *(Feigning dismay.)* Does that mean, dear lady, that I am not upright at all times?

JUNE. I certainly hope not. *(Assumes a pose.)* Oh, yes... *(pretends she is reading a dance card.)* I see that this dance is your's. *(He holds out his arms, she twirls into them, then scoots away.)* Catch me if you can. *(Briefly, laughing, they play "cat and mouse." Finally, breathless, he holds out his arms, she melts into them. As they dance* **JUNE** *glances up and whispers.)* Martha is behind the curtain. *(**HE** starts to look up,)* Don't look! If she senses we've seen her she'll be upset. It's best I go in. And tomorrow...

RODNEY. No, no, we'll wait until I receive my funds. That would be best.

JUNE. Perhaps. I'll take just a wee bit from the cookie jar and we'll go to the cinema and hold hands.

RODNEY. And hold hands. Tonight as I lie abed I shall dream of the touch of your dear soft white hand where I should like to place a... *(Lifts her left hand, kisses the ring finger.)* Until the morrow. *(Turns, exits stage right.)*

JUNE. My little white hand where he would like to place a... *(Twirls joyously, suddenly stops, turns to audience, whispers.)* Is she up there? Is she watching? *(Turning upstage to the window where she fears* **MARTHA** *is watching.)* Oh, Martha, why is it you must walk the floor at night waiting for me to come home? Go back to bed, sister, go back to bed! *(Exits up stage left.)*

(Blue Moon played softly indicates passage of time. The lights dim, slowly rise.)

JUNE. *(Enters stage left. pushing* **VIOLET** *in the wheel chair. She tucks a soft lavender blanket around* **VIOLET***'s legs and points to the sky.)* Look, love, that naughty old sun is hiding behind a cloud.

MARTHA. *(Enters stage left to call from what is the entrance to the house.)* Are you warm enough Violet? Aunt June and I are changing sheets. We won't be long.

JUNE. *(Joining* **MARTHA** *at the door whispers.)* Did she wet the bed?

MARTHA. Yes.

JUNE. Poor pet.

MARTHA. She tried to get to the commode. I found her on the floor.

JUNE. I've told her she must call me.

MARTHA. You would not have heard. You weren't home yet. *(Turns abruptly, enters the house.)*

JUNE. *(Returns to* **VIOLET***, kisses her on the head.)* I'll bring you a biscuit. *(Follows* **MARTHA** *into the house.)*

(Blue Moon is played on the piano with one finger)

VIOLET. *(Lifts her head.)* The aunties see Violet sitting in a wheel chair, mama. "Poor Violet," they say. When you look down from heaven do you see Violet dancing? The Violet with roses in her hair dancing in the meadow on white winter nights? The Violet whose feet don't touch the ground? *(Raises her arms and begins to sway, her face is luminous.)* The Violet made of nothing but light?

JUNE. *(Enters.)* I've brought you a biscuit, sweetheart. Let me wipe your hands. *(Wipes* **VIOLET***'s hands, mimes giving her the biscuit.)* Oh, Violet, your aunties' hearts would burst with joy if you could but say, "Thank you," as you once did. *(Kneels down, lifts* **VIOLET***'s hands, kissing each* *palm.)* Some day you'll speak to us again, won't you, love? *(Rises.)* Someday. *(Exits into the house.)*

VIOLET. The aunties do not hear Violet singing her song, mama...

MARTHA. *(Enters.)* Sheets are changed and I've made you a cup of peppermint tea. And a cracker spread with mayonnaise. *(Mimes setting a cup and plate on a table.)* Come, dear, you must eat. You're nothing but skin and bones.

VIOLET. *(Holding dolly to her breast sings softly, her face alight.)* Singing her song...

MARTHA. *(Sinks into her rocker, sighs.)* A long day. To be expected when you're head of a department. Little wonder I don't sleep at night with all the bills to pay. What would happen if I should sicken? Your Auntie June is inside fussing with her face without a care in the world. No doubt she's reddening her cheeks. Rouge. Mother wouldn't let her out of the house. But what are we to do, you and I?

JUNE. *(Appears at the door flustered.)* I've a run in my hose. Do you have an extra pair?

MARTHA. Yes.

JUNE. May I borrow them?

MARTHA. No.

JUNE. Martha, please.

MARTHA. You're careless.

JUNE. Please.

MARTHA. Oh, alright.

JUNE. You're a dear. Look down the street. Do you see him?

MARTHA. *(Peers down the street.)* He's not in sight. *(JUNE exits. MARTHA turns to VIOLET.)* Every evening asking me to dance. I feel the fool.

VIOLET. *(Shakes Dolly.)* The fool...

MARTHA. *(Sinks into the rocker.)* He's a charmer, yes, but can we trust him? I take a turn or two to keep things pleasant. And I do believe I'm light on my feet.

VIOLET. *(Bouncing dolly.)* Light on my feet...

MARTHA. When father was alive and we went out in society my dance card was always filled. *(Glancing down the street.)* Auntie June had better hurry. He's always on time, I'll give him that. *(Pinches her cheeks.)* Mother approved of pinching our cheeks to give us a bit of color. Do you like Aunt Martha's slippers, dear? They're not new, but I've seldom worn them.

RODNEY. *(Enters stage left, whistling Blue Moon. Mimes climbing the steps.)* Good evening, lovely ladies. What a joy to walk down the avenue, neighbors sitting on porches nodding pleasantly as you pass. The scent of roses. Maple leaves shadowing the sidewalk and the whirl of sprinklers watering the lawns. And the company of charming ladies in a charming town.

MARTHA. Good evening, Mr. Egan.

RODNEY. Rodney, please.

MARTHA. It is a charming town. Where do you call home... Rodney?

RODNEY. Wherever I set my suitcase. My business calls me hither and thither, from where winter lasts until June to where the natives know no winter. But never have I been tempted to linger until now. *(Moves to **MARTHA** and bows.)* A turn or two while we wait for your sister?

MARTHA. No, no.

RODNEY. Please. *(He holds out his arms. She hesitates, rises. They begin to dance.)* Your aunt is light on her feet, Miss Violet, light on her feet.

MARTHA. Some said I was as light as a summer breeze when I waltzed at the cotillion.

RODNEY. Let us be bold. *(He swings her at arm's length and twirls her around. Startled, she falls into his arms as **JUNE** enters.)*

JUNE. *(With a stiff smile.)* You've made my sister laugh. She so seldom laughs, poor dear. *(Turns to **VIOLET**)* I've prepared a custard, sweetheart. You're to eat it before you retire. And I've scented your pillow with lavender. *(Takes* **RODNEY***'s arm possessively.)* I'm sorry I kept you waiting. Shall we go?

RODNEY. The evening is ours.

JUNE. Yes, the evening is ours. *(Turns to* **MARTHA***.)* Don't forget Violet's custard. *(To* **RODNEY** *as they leave.)* She's so forgetful. But then she's so much older than I.

RODNEY. *(Turns to* **MARTHA** *and* **VIOLET***.)* Good evening, ladies. *(Clicks his heels. They exit stage right.)*

MARTHA. So much older? Not quite three years! And my memory is excellent! *(Rises and scans the sky.)* Clouds. The wind is rising. Perhaps it will rain. Your Aunt June didn't take an umbrella. She curls her hair with strips of cloth and she's frantic when caught in the rain. And her custards are frightful.

VIOLET. *(Whispers to dolly.)* Frightful…

MARTHA. I'll make us a tasty pudding. I have our mother's recipe. *(She wheels* **VIOLET** *into the house up left, lights slowly dim. After a moment we hear her call from within.)* Sleep tight, Violet. Sleep tight.

(Music. Lights rise. It's morning. **MARTHA** *enters wheeling* **VIOLET***.)*

MARTHA. I'm sorry I snapped, pet. I didn't sleep well. Walking the floor waiting for your Aunt June to come home. Shameless. Shameless coming home at that hour. I shall not dance with that man again. Bringing her home at such an hour. And the laughter. And the swing squeaking. Back and forth, back and forth. Houses dark the length of the street. I turn off the lights if she isn't home at a decent hour. What will the neighbors think? *(Lowers herself into her rocking chair.)*

JUNE. *(Eenters from the house.)* I baked buns yesterday. You might have left me a bun.

MARTHA. You're not dressed for Sunday Service.

JUNE. I'm not going.

(Silence.)

MARTHA. Please oil the swing.

JUNE. Oil the swing?

MARTHA. The swing squeaks. Oil the swing.

JUNE. You're more handy.

MARTHA. I work while you lounge.

JUNE. Lounge? I cook. I clean. I look after Violet.

MARTHA. And lounge! When I came home ill last December you were sitting on the sofa nibbling chocolate covered cherries. And now you're painting your lips. A woman of your age.

JUNE. And you've been rubbing your cheeks with rose petals! And smiling at Rodney!

MARTHA. Am I not allowed to smile?

JUNE. How many times have I seen you smile since papa's stocks went down?

MARTHA. How many times have I had cause to smile? Standing behind a counter waiting on women who were never invited to a cotillion.

JUNE. And you flutter your eyelashes and dance with him while I'm doing my hair!

MARTHA. I was trying to be pleasant. I expected you to be grateful.

JUNE. Grateful for you turning off the lights so we stumble on the porch steps?

MARTHA. You were raised properly. You should be home by eleven.

JUNE. And you should be in bed asleep, not peeking out of mama's bedroom window!

MARTHA. How can I sleep when I'm not sure he'll bring you home? You're the type of foolish middlc-age woman who might elope.

JUNE. And you're a grim, spiteful spinster fearful a man might lure us out into a world of light and laughter! Why hasn't a window in this house been opened since mama died?

MARTHA. Dust.

JUNE. No!

MARTHA. You don't dust so I don't open windows.

JUNE. You've closed us off from the world!

MARTHA. To protect Violet. The world is not a pretty place.

JUNE. The world is a place of... of possibilities! The possibility of saying your first word, taking your first step, of learning to ride a bike and peddling down the street faster and faster!

MARTHA. And skinning your knees?

JUNE. Yes. And the possibility that someone might be there to kiss my boo-boo.

MARTHA. Who has kissed my boo-boo in the past fifteen years?

JUNE. I have. I've massaged your forehead when you have a headache, and warmed your milk when you can't sleep, and ironed your petticoats and polished your shoes.

MARTHA. So I could work eight hours a day in noise and dust, and deal with cranky dowagers so we could keep this house and care for our Violet! *(***VIOLET** *whimpers.)* More than one young man came to call when I was young, and, yes, I might have wed! But if I had wed you and Violet would be holding out tin cups on some street corner!

JUNE. I could have found work!

MARTHA. And left our Violet alone in the house all day? No! I sacrificed my happiness to care for you both! And what is the thanks I get? Worrying myself into an early grave for fear you might marry that dreadful man and leave!

*(***VIOLET** *begins to cry softly.)*

JUNE. Oh, sister, look what we've done! *(Hastens to* **VIOLET***.)* It's alright, sweetheart... *(Moves behind* **MARTHA***'s rocker, gently touches her older sister's cheek.)* Martha...

MARTHA. *(Slapping* **JUNE***'s hand.)* Don't touch me!

JUNE. *(Sinks to the floor at* **MARTHA***'s feet.* **MARTHA** *stiffens as*

JUNE *rests her head on her knee.)* I'm so sorry. *(**MARTHA**, grim faced, does not respond.)*

VIOLET. *(Barely audible.)* Mama…

*(A long silence. **JUNE** rises and crosses to **VIOLET**.)*

JUNE. Aunt Martha takes good care of us, doesn't she, sweetheart? How could she think I'd leave you?

VIOLET. *(Clutching dolly.)* Leave you…

JUNE. *(Smoothing **VIOLET**'s hair.)* My friend Rodney travels a good deal, little one, and this is a big house. Perhaps we could rent him a room for when he's in town. And there would be a bit of money coming in. We could throw open the windows and fill the house with flowers. *(Turns to **MARTHA**, whose face remains bitter. Moving stage right she peers down the street before finally speaking.)* He's leaving town.

MARTHA. What?

JUNE. He's leaving town.

MARTHA. When?

JUNE, This morning.

MARTHA. No!

JUNE. The eleven o'clock bus.

MARTHA. *(Jumps to her feet.)* What time is it?

JUNE. *(Lifts the small gold watch which hangs on a chain around her neck.)* Twenty minutes to eleven.

MARTHA. You've time! Sister, you have time!

JUNE. Time?

MARTHA. Time to stop him! *(**JUNE** is stunned.)* Don't send your suitor away as I did mine! Don't send away that foolish door-to-door salesman who seems to delight you!

JUNE. I'm wearing my bedroom slippers! It's the Sabbath and I have no hat!

MARTHA. No matter! Hurry! *(Pulls **JUNE** to her feet.)* Hurry, sister! *(Gives **JUNE** a push. **JUNE** runs stage right, stops, whirls to face **MARTHA**.)* Run! *(Firming her slippers on her* *feet* **JUNE** *runs off stage right.)*

MARTHA. *(Watches* **JUNE** *hurry down the street, turns to* **VIOLET**.*)* Do I dare, do I dare open a window? The one in the parlor? How long has it been since a gentleman sat in our parlor? I might cut a few roses. Your grandmother always had a bouquet of roses by the parlor door. Aunt June has never invited Mr. Egan into the house, has she? Perhaps if we open a window… You and I haven't missed Sabbath service since mother passed, Violet, dear, but today we shall be very, very bad doing our very best to be very, very good.

VIOLET. *(Singing while rocking dolly.)* Very, very good… …

MARTHA. *(Sinks into her rocker. Blue Moon plays softly as* **JUNE** *and* **RODNEY** *enter stage right, holding hands and singing.)* Singing on the Sabbath?

RODNEY. Making a joyful noise unto the Lord. Thank you, dear lady. I understand you might rent me a room. *(Crosses to* **VIOLET**.*)* I have taken a turn with your two delightful aunts, Miss Violet. And now… *(He bows.)* I would be honored to take a turn with you. *(***MARTHA** *and* **JUNE** *are aghast.)* If your aunts will sing, softly of course, it being the Sabbath… *(He lifts* **VIOLET***'s hand, kisses it, moves behind the wheel chair, grasps its handles, nods to the two older women.)*

(The sisters stare at each other. **MARTHA** *hesitates, then begins singing Blue Moon in a high, thin voice. As* **JUNE** *joins her* **RODNEY** *swings the chair gently across the porch in time to the music.* **VIOLET**, *her face suffused with joy, lifts her arms and waves them gracefully. The sisters are mesmerized.* **RODNEY** *finally returns the chair to its original position and bows to* **VIOLET**.*)*

It was a pleasure, Miss Violet.

VIOLET. *(Looking up at* **RODNEY** *with a glowing face she struggles to speak, finally managing to say just two words.)* Thank… you…

*(***MARTHA** *and* **JUNE** *are ecstatic, weeping with. joy. At the count of five all four actors hold their positions as if*

caught in a still life photograph. After another count of five they bow and exit.)

End of Play

COSTUME PLOT

MARTHA wears a plain black dress.

JUNE wears a pink dress with full skirt and a small gold watch on a chain around her neck.

VIOLET wears a filmy white dress.

RODNEY wears a blue suit, white shirt and flowered tie.

PROPERTY PLOT

A lavender blanket and doll with porcelain face. Both MARTHA and JUNE mime carrying tidbits of food on stage for VIOLET.

SET PLOT

Two white wicker rockers sit left of center. VIOLET is wheeled on and off stage in a small wheel chair. Down stage right are several large containers containing pink roses and purple petunias.

I REMEMBER HEAVEN, OF COURSE

A PLAY IN ONE ACT

CAST OF CHARACTERS

DORA – A whimsical woman seventy five years of age.
ALICE ANNE – Her daughter.
REILLY – Dora's doctor.
Alice Anne and Reilly also play the parts of several other characters as voices remembered.

SCENE

The action takes place on a bare stage but for an old upholstered rocking chair stage center.

TIME

The time is the present.

DORA *enters stage left. A pretty older woman she wears a filmy pastel flowered dress. Her hair curls softly around her face.*

ALICE ANNE *enters down stage left wearing a blue skirt and white blouse, her hair tied back with a red ribbon as* **REILLY** *enters down stage right wearing a blue suit, white shirt and red tie.* **THEY** *remain standing far downstage as they speak as various characters.* **DORA** *looks at neither during the play for their voices are voices remembered.*

DORA. I remember heaven, of course. Having been there, that is. But I simply cannot remember the name of the book I borrowed from the library last week. *(Moving stage right.)* Now where did I put it? *(Mimes checking books in a bookcase.)* Not in the bookcase, no.

ALICE ANNE. *(To the audience.)* Mother's short term memory is deplorable.

DORA. ...Alice Anne says. But my long term memory is nothing less than extraordinary. I haven't the slightest difficulty remembering that wondrous realm my soul inhabited before dropping plop into my mother's womb.

ALICE ANNE. Don't listen to a word she says.

DORA. "Damn," I remember thinking, here I go again! Even as an embryo I remembered other less than successful incarnations. And I did so yearn to remain in paradise where once a year a dinner is served of nothing but strawberry shortcake.

ALICE ANNE. I'm embarrassed to take her to church.

DORA. But as usual I did something naughty.

REILLY. *(In a deep voice as from heaven.)* Now try to behave properly!

DORA. ...I heard St. Peter call as my soul hurtled through space. And what did I do? I began this current lifetime swearing like a trouper.

REILLY. *(Calling.)* Will you never learn?

DORA. Those were the last words I heard that good Saint say. Will I never learn?

ALICE ANNE. You simply must behave properly when you're with the children.

DORA. ...Alice Anne said only this morning. Alice Anne, my daughter, overheard me telling little Daniel that heaven is a place for saints and fools where no one cuts their toenails and even Jehovah breaks the rules.

ALICE ANNE. Oh, mother!

DORA. ...My daughter said.

ALICE ANNE. Will you never learn?

DORA. And picking up her gardening gloves Alice Anne slammed out the back door to supervise little Daniel who was playing in the kiddie pool.

ALICE ANNE. *(Calls.)* Keep your bathing suit on, Daniel.

DORA. ...I heard her say.

ALICE ANNE. That's the rule!

DORA. Alice Anne sets great store in obeying the rules. *(Turning to look off stage right.)* Was that the door? *(Moves stage right. On tiptoe mimes peering out a window.)* No one there. Must be my hearing. Alice Anne scolds me for turning up the television.

ALICE. *(Calling.)* Turn down the television!

DORA. Fiddle de de. Now where did I put that book?

REILLY. *(With the voice of a small child.)* Grandma?

DORA. *(Mimes seeing Daniel run into the room)* Don't run, Daniel, you'll slip! Gracious, you're soaking wet! Let me wipe your face. *(Mimes taking a handkerchief from her pocket and wiping his face.)*

REILLY. *(As Daniel.)* Grandma?

DORA. Yes, dear?

REILLY. *(As Daniel.)* Grandma, I couldn't see the goblin under the butterfly bush.

DORA. Were you looking with your eyes wide open?

REILLY. *(As Daniel.)* Yes.

DORA. To see a goblin you must close your eyes.

REILLY. *(As Daniel.)* I can't see with my eyes closed.

DORA. We only see goblins, and elves and magical beings under a butterfly bush when we're not looking. But you're five years old. Grandma didn't see a goblin until she was seven. So after lunch we'll sit under the butterfly bush and I'll see him when we're not looking and describe that merry little fellow.

ALICE ANNE. *(Calling as from the garden.)* Daniel? Where are you?

DORA. Run out to the pool now, mama likes to keep an eye on you. *(Mimes watching Daniel run to the kitchen.)* He's a darling. When he gets to heaven he'll put in a good word for me. Now where did I put that book? My mind has been spinning since Alice Anne scolded me. And in front of little Daniel.

ALICE ANNE. No one cuts their toenails! What nonsense!

DORA. Of course it was nonsense. But how else is one to remind the little dear of the Elysian Fields from whence he came? That realm of innocence where teddy bears eat honey with their furry little paws and peacocks peck and preen. And Daniel does so love strawberry shortcake and does so hate to have his toenails cut. And as for rules, adults don't seem to remember that even God has second thoughts.

ALICE ANNE. *(To the audience.)* She says such things to neighbors! I hear them laughing over the clothes lines!

DORA. Fiddle de dum... Oh, yes, the book. The cover was red as I recall. And what was the name? Written by some fellow who got himself into trouble. And as for all that twaddle about the meaning of life? Poof! If the author can't remember from whence he came how can he tell us where we're headed? What else matters at my age? I don't celebrate birthdays anymore, but Alice Anne tells others I'm seventy five. She ought not do that, but then I don't suppose I should tell them she colors her hair. Seventy five?

ALICE ANNE. Yes, you're seventy five.

DORA. I can't possibly be seventy five. Every time she says such a thing I have to sit down. *(Sinking into the rocking chair and placing her hand over her heart.)* Oh, dear. Thump, thump, thump.

ALICE ANNE. Doctor Reilly has told her not to fuss.

REILLY. *(As Dr. Reilly in a rich, melodious voice.)* You're not to fret, young lady.

DORA. …That dratted man will say! *(Rising.)* Who is he to tell me not to fret? But since he was William's best friend he feels he has the right to pop in whenever he pleases. Twenty minutes after I've put brownies in the oven he's at the front door.

ALICE ANNE. How can you be so ungracious?

DORA. Alice Anne says I'm ungracious.

ALICE ANNE. He was daddy's best friend!

DORA. …She reminds me.

ALICE. And you sit him at the kitchen table with a mug of tea when you know he'd prefer a cup of freshly brewed black coffee served in the parlor! And he practically has to beg you for a brownie! Why are you so wicked?

DORA. Why am I so wicked? Why a mug of tea in the kitchen? Why, indeed! Because he insists on telling me William was a saint! And Alice Anne sings the same song.

REILLY. That man was a saint.

DORA. Meaning, of course, that any man who would marry me had to be a saint!

ALICE ANNE. Daddy was a darling.

DORA. But not a saint! *(Gasps.)* Oh, dear. When I raise my voice it sets my heart to pumping. *(To the audience.)* How would you feel if when you get to heaven you find your husband wearing a halo?

(The ring of a phone.)

ALICE ANNE. *(Mimes picking up a receiver. Then speaks in the high, thin voice of an elderly church lady.)* Alice Anne, I'm calling as chairman of the used clothing drive. Please come to the church as soon as possible and pick up the items your mother dropped off. You'll find them in the church basement in a plain brown wrapper.

DORA. Did they think I wore flannel? I'd go to bed wearing nothing but my lavender cologne if I had nothing but flannel! Now where did I put that book. In the bookcase? *(Moves stage right to mime looking in the bookcase)* No, no, I do believe I looked in the bookcase. *(To the audience.)* I looked in the bookcase, didn't I? Oh, dear, perhaps Alice Anne is humoring me. Perhaps I actually am seventy five!

ALICE ANNE. *(To the audience.)* What am I to do?

DORA. Do you suppose I'm really a bad influence on the children? Daniel had a snit when he learned Adam ran around the garden wearing nothing but a fig leaf while he has to wear scratchy trousers to Sunday school. I assured him that when he gets to heaven he, too, can wear a fig leaf.

ALICE ANNE. A fig leaf? Either she's having a breakdown or I am!

REILLY. A bit of fine port before bed will settle your mother's nerves.

ALICE ANNE. But what will settle mine?

DORA. All I tell little Daniel is true, metaphorically speaking. But as Alice Anne is adverse to metaphors, she tends to have a snit. *(Giggles.)* I tended to cause a snit or two in heaven.

REILLY. *(As SAINT PETER calls.)* It's no laughing matter!

DORA. *(Looking up.)* Not on purpose! *(Whispers to the audience.)* Certainly not on purpose. Oh, dear, listen to my heart.

ALICE ANNE. *(Concerned.)* Sit down, mama.

DORA. Best to sit down and rock. *(Sitting.)* It feels good to lower myself into this old chair. Alice Anne wants to buy me a new one. Why would I want a new one?

ALICE ANNE. It squeaks!

DORA. Three generations have rocked in this chair at the end of the day reading the Good Book. I may cuss a little, but I read the Good Book. I remind St. Peter it sits on my bedside table when he finds me putting chewing gum behind my headboard and has a snit.

ALICE ANNE. Only children put chewing gum behind their head board. But mother has never grown up.

REILLY. Younger than springtime. *(Breathes deeply.)* And, ah, that lavender cologne.

DORA. *(To the audience.)* I started chewing gum when I stopped smoking. When I stopped chewing gum I started biting my nails. *(Examines her nails.)* Now that I've stopped biting my nails I have the strangest dreams. Not unpleasant, but very strange. Do you believe in reincarnation?

ALICE ANNE. Mother!

DORA. Dozing of late I find myself wandering in strangely familiar landscapes living strangely familiar lives.

ALICE ANNE. Isn't the life you're living strange enough?

DORA. Do you suppose this a punishment for those less then successful incarnations. What comes to mind, of course, was that 15th century debacle when I find myself banished from the monastery for doing something unseemly. *(Rocks a moment.)* Do you smell the roses? The back door must be open.

REILLY. *(As Daniel calling from the kiddy pool.)* I'm making waves, mama! Whoopee!

DORA. Whoopee, indeed, Daniel, "a merry heart doeth good like a medicine." *(Taking a deep breath she leans back and closes her eyes.)* There is nothing like the scent of wild roses warm in the sun. *(Rocks gently.)*

ALLICE ANNE & REILLY. *(Together say softly.)* Roses warm in the sun.

REILLY. *(As Daniel.)* Grandma, I couldn't see the goblin under the butterfly bush.

DORA. Were you looking with your eyes wide open?

REILLY. *(As Daniel.)* Yes.

DORA. To see a goblin you must close your eyes.

REILLY. *(As Daniel.)* I can't see with my eyes closed.

DORA. We only see goblins, and elves and magical beings under a butterfly bush when we're not looking. But you're five years old. Grandma didn't see a goblin until she was seven. So after lunch we'll sit under the butterfly bush and I'll see him when we're not looking and describe that merry little fellow.

ALICE ANNE. *(Calling as from the garden.)* Daniel? Where are you?

DORA. Run out to the pool now, mama likes to keep an eye on you. *(Mimes watching Daniel run to the kitchen.)* He's a darling. When he gets to heaven he'll put in a good word for me. Now where did I put that book? My mind has been spinning since Alice Anne scolded me. And in front of little Daniel.

ALICE ANNE. No one cuts their toenails! What nonsense!

DORA. Of course it was nonsense. But how else is one to remind the little dear of the Elysian Fields from whence he came? That realm of innocence where teddy bears eat honey with their furry little paws and peacocks peck and preen. And Daniel does so love strawberry shortcake and does so hate to have his toenails cut. And as for rules, adults don't seem to remember that even God has second thoughts.

ALICE ANNE. *(To the audience.)* She says such things to neighbors! I hear them laughing over the clothes lines!

DORA. Fiddle de dum... Oh, yes, the book. The cover was red as I recall. And what was the name? Written by some fellow who got himself into trouble. And as for all that twaddle about the meaning of life? Poof! If the author can't remember from whence he came how can he tell us where we're headed? What else matters at my age? I don't celebrate birthdays anymore, but Alice Anne tells others I'm seventy five. She ought not do that, but then I don't suppose I should tell them she colors her hair. Seventy five?

ALICE ANNE. Yes, you're seventy five.

DORA. I can't possibly be seventy five. Every time she says such a thing I have to sit down. *(Sinking into the rocking chair and placing her hand over her heart.)* Oh, dear. Thump, thump, thump.

ALICE ANNE. Doctor Reilly has told her not to fuss.

REILLY. *(As Dr. Reilly in a rich, melodious voice.)* You're not to fret, young lady.

DORA. …That dratted man will say! *(Rising.)* Who is he to tell me not to fret? But since he was William's best friend he feels he has the right to pop in whenever he pleases. Twenty minutes after I've put brownies in the oven he's at the front door.

ALICE ANNE. How can you be so ungracious?

DORA. Alice Anne says I'm ungracious.

ALICE ANNE. He was daddy's best friend!

DORA. …She reminds me.

ALICE. And you sit him at the kitchen table with a mug of tea when you know he'd prefer a cup of freshly brewed black coffee served in the parlor! And he practically has to beg you for a brownie! Why are you so wicked?

DORA. Why am I so wicked? Why a mug of tea in the kitchen? Why, indeed! Because he insists on telling me William was a saint! And Alice Anne sings the same song.

REILLY. That man was a saint.

DORA. Meaning, of course, that any man who would marry me had to be a saint!

ALICE ANNE. Daddy was a darling.

DORA. But not a saint! *(Gasps.)* Oh, dear. When I raise my voice it sets my heart to pumping. *(To the audience.)* How would you feel if when you get to heaven you find your husband wearing a halo?

ALICE ANNE. He was loved and admired.

REILLY. A saint.

DORA. I was not married to a saint! Saints don't itch. And the summer Will caught poison ivy he scratched till he bled!

REILLY. Now, now, little lady, I've told you not to fret.

DORA. ...That pesky man croons. What school would give him a medical degree? When I told him I suspect he wears a stethoscope to bed he said he'd be happy to give me the opportunity to prove it! When I asked him where he got his degree he chuckled. *(*REILLY *chuckles.)* So I told him I'd ask Marcelia Hall. I suspect she knows what he wears to bed...

ALICE ANNE. Mother, Marcelia is your friend!

REILLY. A lovely lady, Marcelia.

DORA. ...He insists on telling me. And he expects me to serve him coffee in a porcelain cup and plump up the cushions in the parlor so he can rest his gouty foot on great-grandmother's needlepoint when he spends every Saturday evening drinking fine port on Marcelia Hall's front porch.

(The sound of a phone.)

DORA. The phone. Where is the phone? *(Scurries around looking for the phone. Mimes finding it and picking up the receiver.)* Hello.

ALICE ANNE. *(As MARCELIA, speaking in a low dramatic voice.)* Dora?

DORA. Yes.

ALICE ANNE. This is Marcelia. Dr. Reilly just called to tell me I got the part!

DORA. No!

ALICE ANNE. Yes!

DORA. It pays to serve a fine port, doesn't it, Marcelia? *(Mimes slamming down the receiver.)* As the director of our community theater that pompous ass cast Marcelia in the leading role in a production of Arsenic and Old Lace. Everyone agreed I should have had the role!

REILLY. Now, now Dora, there's a dandy little role for you. You'll steal the show.

DORA. And I did!

ALICE ANNE *(As herself.)* With your outrageous makeup! You should be ashamed of yourself!

REILLY. *(Teasing.)* If you had but served a fine port, dear Dora.

DORA. ...That damn man insists on saying. Ooh! *(To the audience.)* Did I swear? I did, didn't I? *(Looking up.)* I hope he didn't hear me.

REILLY. *(As SAINT PETER.)* I heard!

DORA. Will I never learn?

ALICE ANNE. Daddy had his doubts.

DORA. Dear William...

REILLY. Come now, lovely lady, let me listen to your heart.

DORA. He draws me close and rests his ear on my bodice. I smell the peppermint on his breath and give him a shove! *(Mimes shoving* **REILLY.***)* Suppose Alice Anne should walk in!

REILLY. Your little heart goes pitty pat.

DORA. I can't abide that man.

ALICE ANNE. He's so good looking.

DORA. ... Alice Anne insists on saying. *(To* **ALICE ANNE.***)* Poof, I've seen better. And he's too old for me.

ALICE ANNE. Mother, you're seventy five!

DORA. So you say. Others swear I'm ten years younger.

ALICE ANNE. You behave as if you were a twenty five year old with not an ounce of common sense. Imagine my embarrassment when the ladies of the church told me you had dropped off a pair of black lace panties and a scandalous nightie for the yearly used clothing sale.

DORA. *(Looking up.)* Hush! He might hear!

REILLY. *(As Saint Peter.)* I heard!

DORA. The other afternoon as I dozed off I heard myself murmur the word, "Jerusalem."

ALICE ANNE & REILLY. *(Together, softly.)* Jerusalem.

DORA. Words have always glowed with color. The word Jerusalem is golden. Not the gold of a cold hard coin, the gold of sunset over the Dead Sea.

ALICE ANN. *(Softly.)* The gold of sunset...

REILLY. *(Softly.)* ... Over the Dead Sea.

DORA. My shoulders began to ache. As I leaned back it was as if I was soaking up the heat of an old stone wall. A wall that had baked in the sun for a thousand years.

ALICE & REILLY. *(Together, softly.)* A thousand years.

DORA. And yet I've never been to Jerusalem. And in the dream I saw men in brightly colored robes of scarlet and blue walking up the steps to the temple door.

REILLY. *(Softly.)* Robes of scarlet...

ALICE ANNE. *(Softly.)* ... And robes of blue.

REILLY. *(As Daniel.)* Grandma?

ALICE ANNE. *(To the audience.)* Daniel had entered the room.

REILLY. *(As Daniel.)* Grandma, are you dead?

ALICE ANNE. *(To the audience.)* Daniel, bathing suit dripping, wiggled his little body between my mother's knees.

REILLY. *(As DANIEL.)* Are you in heaven, grandma?

ALICE ANNE. ... He whispered..

DORA. I opened my eyes and found myself looking into the upturned face of a child. Daniel?

ALICE ANNE. ...He nodded.

DORA. No, no, darling, I managed to say. I don't believe I'm dead. Daydreaming? Yes, I do believe I was daydreaming. Daniel looked relieved. I was somewhat relieved myself. I tapped him on the nose. You know what?

REILLY. *(As Daniel.)* What?

DORA. I'm so happy to be here with my grandson. *(Miming.)* And I wrapped my arms around that little wet body and drew him on to my lap. I do believe I shall make strawberry shortcake for dinner tonight.

REILLY. *(As Daniel.)* Whoopee!

DORA. Whoopee, indeed. You shall sprinkle the berries with powdered sugar and mash them.

DANIEL. Mash them!

DORA. And when you've mashed the berries. *(Mimes mashing the berries.)* I'll mix the sugared berries with heavy cream. None of that whipped cream out of a can, no, no, but heavy cream fresh from the dairy. And if we should like a second bowl we shall have a second bowl.

REILLY. *(As Daniel.)* And if I want three bowls of strawberry shortcake, Grandma?

DORA You shall have three bowls! And we whooped with joy!

REILLY. *(As Daniel.)* Whoopee!

(At the count of five they lower their eyes and remain immobile as if pictured in a still photograph.)

End of Play

COSTUME PLOT

DORA wears a pastel flowered dress.

ALICE ANNE wears a blue skirt, white shirt, her hair tied back with a red ribbon.

REILLY wears a blue suit, white shirt and red tie.

PROPERTY PLOT

Set properties as well as personal properties are mimed.

SET PLOT

The stage is empty but for an old upholstered rocking chair stage center.

Also by
Jean Lenox Toddie...

And Go to Innisfree
And Send Forth a Raven
A Bag of Green Apples
By the Name of Kensington
Is that the Bus to Pittsburgh?
The Juice of Wild Strawberries
Late Sunday Afternoon, Early Sunday Evening
A Little Something for the Ducks
Lookin' for a Better Berry Bush
Scent of Honeysuckle
The Silver Apples of the Moon
Tell Me Another Story, Sing Me a Song
Those Singing Sunday Mornings
White Room of My Remembering

Please visit our website **samuelfrench.com** for complete descriptions and licensing information

www.ingramcontent.com/pod-product-compliance
Lightning Source LLC
Chambersburg PA
CBHW070649300426
44111CB00013B/2339